D0647818

Kimi Shiruya-

Dost thou Know?

KAZE KITARU - THE WIND COMETH
3
AO FUKASHI - DEEP GREEN
47
MICHI YUKABA - DOWN THIS ROAD
89
DOST THOU KNOW
117
AUTHOR'S NOTE
170

Translation	**Sachiko Sato**
Lettering	**Melanie Lewis**
Graphic Design	**Eric Rosenberger**
Editing	**Stephanie Donnelly**
Editor in Chief	**Fred Lui**
Publisher	**Hikaru Sasahara**

KIMI SHIRUYA - DOST THOU KNOW? © SATORU ISHIHARA 2003. Originally published in Japan in 2003 by SHINSHOKAN CO., LTD. English translation rights arranged through TOHAN CORPORATION, TOKYO. All rights reserved. English translation copyright © 2005 by DIGITAL MANGA, Inc. All other material © 2005 by DIGITAL MANGA, Inc. All rights reserved. No portion of this publication may be reproduced or transmitted in any form or by any means without written permission from the copyright holders. Any likeness of characters, places, and situations featured in this publication to actual persons (living or deceased), events, places, and situations is purely coincidental. The JUNÉ logo is ™ of DIGITIAL MANGA, Inc.

English Edition Published by
DIGITAL MANGA PUBLISHING
A division of DIGITAL MANGA, Inc.
1487 W 178th Street, Suite 300
Gardena, CA 90248

www.dmpbooks.com

First Edition: October 2005
ISBN: 1-56970-934-3

3 5 7 9 10 8 6 4 2

Printed in China

WHAP
KAZE KITARU- THE WIND COMETH
WINNER-
TSUKISHIMA MUNICIPAL HIGH SCHOOL SECOND YEAR STUDENT, KATSUOMI HANAMORI!
JUDGEMENT! RED!
青海八重樫
SEIKAI YAEGASHI
HANAMORI

風来る
KAZE KITARU - THE WIND COMETH

GLARE
YOU LOST—
DIDN'T YOU, KID.
BIG BRO!
SHUT UP, MASAOMI.
WHY CAN'T I WIN AGAINST HIM, DAMMIT?!
ARRGH! THAT DAMN YOUNGER YAEGASHI! HE LOOKS LIKE SUCH A GIRL BUT HE BEAT ME!
IF YOU'RE A REAL MAN, GO FOR THE BIGGEST ONE!
WHAT'S WITH THIS TINY CUP?
WINNER, HIGH SCHOOL DIVISION.
SECOND PLACE, JUNIOR HIGH DIVISION.

YOU!
きっ
GLOWER
さっ
SLINK
HERE THEY ARE - THE YAEGASHI BROTHERS.
DID YOU SEE THAT? YAEGASHI— JUST NOW...!
HE LOOKED TOWARD YOU AND MADE A "HMPH" FACE, BRO.
IT CAN'T BE HELPED...

FUDOU SHOPPING DISTRICT
POPS SAID HE'D HAVE IT READY... THE BEST TUNA IN TSUKIJI!
THE CELEBRATORY BOAT-DISPLAY SUSHI -
LET'S GO.
A STRONG MAN ALSO HAS MANY ENEMIES.
MR. YAEGASHI
NONE?! WHY?!
AND-AND IT SAYS "YAEGASHI"...
THE CUSTOMER COMES FIRST.
...FOR A HOUSE-WARMING PARTY OVER ON FIRST STREET.
ZAA
IT CAN'T BE HELPED. WE GOT AN ORDER...
花森鮮魚店
HANAMORI FISH STORE

YOU DON'T HAVE TO GO, BRO!
THE ORDER MAY BE FOR OUR ARCH-RIVALS!
HELL-OOO -
I'LL JUST GO HAVE A LOOK.
KATSUOMI, MAKE A QUICK DELIVERY RUN, WILL YA?
RIGHT.
SORRY, WE'RE ALREADY CLOSED FOR TODAY.
PARDON ME...
HM?
OH—

YOU DON'T HAVE TO RUN AWAY AT THE SIGHT OF MY FACE...
TCH
GOOD TIMING... I WAS JUST ABOUT TO DELIV—
DASH
HUH? HEY!
OK, I'M OFF.
RING RING
花森鮮魚店
HANAMORI FISH STORE
大田精

きっ
SKREEK
THAT YOU?
YAE-GASHI!

SUR-PRISED YOU, DIDN'T HE?
HE'S SO TIMID...

SO I HEAR YOU MOVED IN.
...WHERE ON FIRST STREET?
THERE.

...YEAH.
MY LITTLE BROTHER JUST NOW—
SORRY ABOUT THAT.

I GO TO MINATO DOJO AND MY LITTLE BRO GOES TO A PLACE CALLED TSUKISHIMA DOJO.
THEN I'LL GO TO TSUKISHIMA.
EVEN AS THE ENEMY, HE SEEMS LIKE A MUCH NICER GUY THAN I THOUGHT.
RIVER CITY...! YOU RICH KIDS.
IS THERE A KENDO DOJO NEARBY?

...I FEAR IT MIGHT BLUNT MY SWORD SKILLS.
IF I BECOME FRIENDLY WITH YOU...
I TAKE IT BACK!
I DON'T WANT TO GET TOO CLOSE TO YOU.

I'M GOING TO BREACH YOUR DEFENSES.
AT THE NEXT TOURNA-MENT...
HOW TO SAY THIS...
HE RESEM-BLES A SWORD...
THAT YAE-GASHI.
I NEVER EVEN CONSIDERED IT...
...WERE FRIENDS, CLOSER THAN ANY OTHERS?
BUT, WHAT IF WE...
—USS!
MINATO KENDO
湊剣道
—MASS!

SEE THAT YOU ALL DEVOTE YOURSELVES TO PRACTICE.
—USS!
STARTING TODAY, WE WELCOME A NEW STUDENT TO OUR DOJO—
SAYA YAE-GASHI.
HOW WOULD WE FEEL WHEN FACING EACH OTHER IN TOURNAMENT?
AW MAN, NOT HIM!
AT THE LAST TOURNA-MENT...
HE'S THE GUY WHO WON THE JUNIOR HIGH DIVISION!
WHY DOES HE HAVE TO SHOW UP AT OUR DOJO?
HE HAS THAT GIRLY FACE, BUT...
SUDDENLY—BAM! HE STRIKES A GAUNTLET.
SCARY!
LOOM
LET'S JUST IGNORE HIM.
YEAH, IGNORE...

WHAAT? BUT I DON'T WANT TO...
YOU TEAM UP WITH YAEGASHI.
HE TROUNCED ME IN THE LAST TOURNAMENT.
HANAMORI ANGLE

AAH! SIR ULTRAMAN DYNA!
DON'T "SIR DYNA" ME.
SHIMURA.
YOU'RE LOOMING HUGE AS EVER!

HUH?! A LEADER?!
POWER...? YOU THINK SO?
THAT'S RIGHT.
CHUCKLE
BLUSH

SHIMURA.
YOU'RE SEEN AS THE LEADER OF THESE MID-RANK RUNTS, AREN'T YOU?
THE OTHERS WILL FOLLOW YOUR LEAD.
DON'T WASTE SUCH POWER OVER TRIVIAL THINGS.
花森

YAEGASHI!
YES.

DON'T CRY!
COACH HANAMORI NIDAN (SECOND LEVEL) IS BULLYING YAEGASHI...
IF YOU KEEP ACTING TIMID, IT'S JUST GOING TO GET HARDER AND HARDER...
HUH?!
じゅわぁぁ
WHEN SOMETHING LIKE THAT HAPPENS, SPEAK UP FOR YOURSELF!
ABOUT MR. YAEGASHI! THAT MR. TSURUGI!
HE WENT UP AGAINST THE HACHIDAN (EIGHTH LEVEL) DOJO MASTER IN FREE PRACTICE AND SCORED A POINT!
IT WAS SOOO COOL!
WHOAA...
HEY, LISTEN! LISTEN TO THIS!
どたどたどたど

MAN, HE WAS FAST!
LIKE A WIND WHIPPING THROUGH.
IF YOU'RE A TYPHOON, BRO...
THEN HE'S A GALE.
AT THE NEXT TOURNAMENT... I'M GOING TO BREACH YOUR DEFENSES.
A GALE...
DURING THE FINALS... THREE TIMES—
HE LEAPT THROUGH MY FRONT.

THE MA-AI (STRIKING SPACE) I MAINTAINED...
HE SLIPPED RIGHT THROUGH.
A HARU HAYATE (SPRING GALE) -
HUH?
THAT'S WHAT THEY CALL SOMETHING LIKE THAT - A SPRING GALE.
NOT GOOD.
IF I DON'T PROPERLY MAINTAIN MY DEFENSES ...
EVEN NOW, I FEEL LIKE HE'S GOING TO LEAP IN CLOSE TO ME...
GOOD MORNING.

THOSE WERE TEARS OF HAPPINESS, APPARENTLY.
I CAME TO THANK YOU.
MY BAD.
SO, I HEARD YOU MADE MY BROTHER CRY?
SPEAK OF THE DEVIL!
WHAT'RE YOU DOING HERE?
STOP!
CLEAR, RESONANT VOICE.
STRAIGHT AND NOBLE POSTURE.
AT HOME,
WE'VE ALWAYS TREATED SAYA LIKE A FRAGILE THING...
AS HE BECAME SKILLED IN KENDO, IT ONLY MADE THINGS WORSE.
BUT...
...HONESTLY, EVER SINCE HE'S BEEN ATTENDING THE SAME DOJO AS YOU...
MY BROTHER HAS SLOWLY BEGUN TO CHANGE.

AS HIS BIG BROTHER, I'M A LITTLE JEALOUS.
"MY BAD," YOU SAID?
YOU DON'T MAKE EXCUSES, DO YOU.
THERE, AGAIN...
HE CLOSED IN.
WELL, THEN ...
I'M TAKING THE SUBWAY.
IF I COULD, I'D LIKE TO CROSS SWORDS WITH YOU ONE DAY...
THROB
...USING REAL BLADES.

THIS SPRING GALE HAS CAUGHT ME UNAWARE.
WHAT IF—
WHAT IF I FELL IN LOVE WITH HIM...
WOULD MY SKILL WITH THE SHINAI...
'SHTAA!
...BECOME DULLED?

LET'S GO OUT FOR SOME RAMEN.
YOU WERE REALLY INTO IT TODAY—HUH, HANAMORI?
'USS.
YAE-GASHI.
YOU WANNA GO OUT FOR SOME RAMEN ...
WHISH
JUST PUT IT ON!
YOU HURT? HERE, PUT THIS ON.
SLAP
TUG
!
AASH!

THAT'S STRANGE... THOSE BRUISES...
A SHINAI WOULDN'T MAKE THEM THERE...
AND THEN YOU KNOW WHAT MR. TSURUGI DID?!
OWWW!
DON'T MENTION TSURUGI IN FRONT OF ME.
HUH?! WHAT?!
ARE YOU TRYING TO MAKE A MILQUE-TOAST OUT OF ME?!
OH, THAT'S RIGHT... YOU GO TO THE SAME JUNIOR HIGH AS SAYA, DON'T YOU?
KOFF
HACK
KOFF
KOFF
KOFF

PLEASE FORGIVE ME, SIR DYNA!
PING
PING
WHITE
SHAKE SHAKE, SHAKE
WHAT... YOU KNOW SOMETHING, DON'T YOU?
I'VE SEEN HIM GETTING BEATEN UP BEFORE.
THE SENIORS DO IT ALL THE TIME.
NEW KIDS ALWAYS GET THE TREATMENT.
BUT THEY USUALLY STOP AFTER LIKE TWO OR THREE TIMES, TOPS.

BUT WE'RE IN DIFFERENT CLASSES...
"BUT" NOTHING!
AND YOU JUST STOOD BY AND WATCHED?
HE'S GOT BRUISES IN DIFFERENT PLACES EVERY DAY.
YOU SURE?
ISN'T THAT HOW YOU ARE?
IF YOU'RE STILL HOLDING A GRUDGE FOR LOSING TO HIM IN THE TOURNA-MENT...
YOU'RE MAKING A HUGE MISTAKE.
STILL, WHY SHOULD I...
DAMN ...
WHY DO I HAVE TO STICK MY NECK OUT FOR HIM?

TSURUGI DIDN'T SEEM AWARE OF IT EITHER...
SO THE KID'S BEARING IT ON HIS OWN EVERY DAY.
I GUESS THEY'RE RELATED AFTER ALL.
THEY'RE THE SAME AT HEART.
OH, NO!!
I'M THINKING ABOUT TSURUGI AGAIN!
都立月島中学校
TSUKISHIMA MUNICIPAL JUNIOR HIGH SCHOOL

GUYS! HELP WITH THE CLEANUP!
THEY SURE ARE BOLD TO DO THIS IN THE MIDDLE OF THE SCHOOLYARD.
HEY!
OH MAN, THEY'RE AT IT AGAIN.
ISN'T HE STRONG ...
...LIKE, AT KENDO, OR SOME-THING?
YOU CAN'T USE YOUR KENDO TECHNIQUES FOR SOMETHING LIKE THAT.
YOU CAN'T DO THAT.
WHY DOESN'T HE JUST BEAT'EM UP WITH, LIKE, A MOP?
SAYA KNOWS THAT... HE UNDER-STANDS!
THERE'D BE WAX ALL OVER THE PLACE.

DUMP
JUST STANDING AROUND LAUGHING— YOU GUYS ARE THE LOWEST!
I'M THE LOWEST, TOOOO!
YEAH, THAT'S RIGHT...
HE UNDER-STANDS THAT...
WHAT'S UP, HANA-MORI?
YOU'RE CREEP-ING US OUT...

I'M HOME.
YO, KATSU... SORRY, BUT COME HELP ME OUT IN THE STORE.
WHERE'S BAKA-OMI?
IT'S HIS TURN TODAY, ISN'T IT?

OH, KATSU YOU'RE WORKING LATE.
THANKS FOR YOUR BUSI-NESS.
CURT AS USUAL, AREN'T YOU?
HA HA HA
SWA~Y
PROBABLY AT THE ARCADE AGAIN.
DAMN HIM. WHEN HE GETS BACK, IT'S PUNISHMENT MODE.
NO, HE WAS ABSENT TODAY.
I SEE... THANKS!
TSURUGI!
HUFF
PUFF
WAS SAYA AT THE DOJO TODAY?!

WHAT'S WRONG? WHAT'S HAPPENED?
SAYA HASN'T COME HOME.
THIS HAS NEVER HAPPENED.
WAIT!
I'VE SEEN HIM GETTING BEATEN UP BEFORE.
RIGHT.
YOU STILL DON'T KNOW THIS AREA, DO YOU?
I'LL GO WITH YOU.
YO, OLD MAN! CLOSE UP FOR ME, WILL YA?!

HANA-MORI...
COME ON.
GUESS WE SHOULD START WITH THE RUNTS' LIKELY HANG-OUTS.
CINE-SWITCH
THE BRUISES ...
MASAOMI TOLD ME ABOUT THEM.
ハンバーガー
SAYA WON'T TELL ME THE CAUSE OF HIS INJURIES, BUT...
I KNEW YOU WERE THE FIRST ONE TO NOTICE.

TSURUGI.
IT'S NO GOOD. THEY HAVEN'T FOUND HIM.
WHAT DID THEY SAY?
...SOMETHING SIMILAR HAPPENED AT HIS PREVIOUS SCHOOL...
THAT'S WHY WE MOVED HERE.
TSURUGI.
MASAOMI MAY BE WITH HIM.
I THINK I HAVE AN IDEA.
HE CAN'T HAVE GONE TO THE RIVER...
LEPHONE
YOUR KID BROTHER ISN'T AS WEAK AS YOU THINK.
HE WAS BEARING HIS BURDEN ALL ALONE.

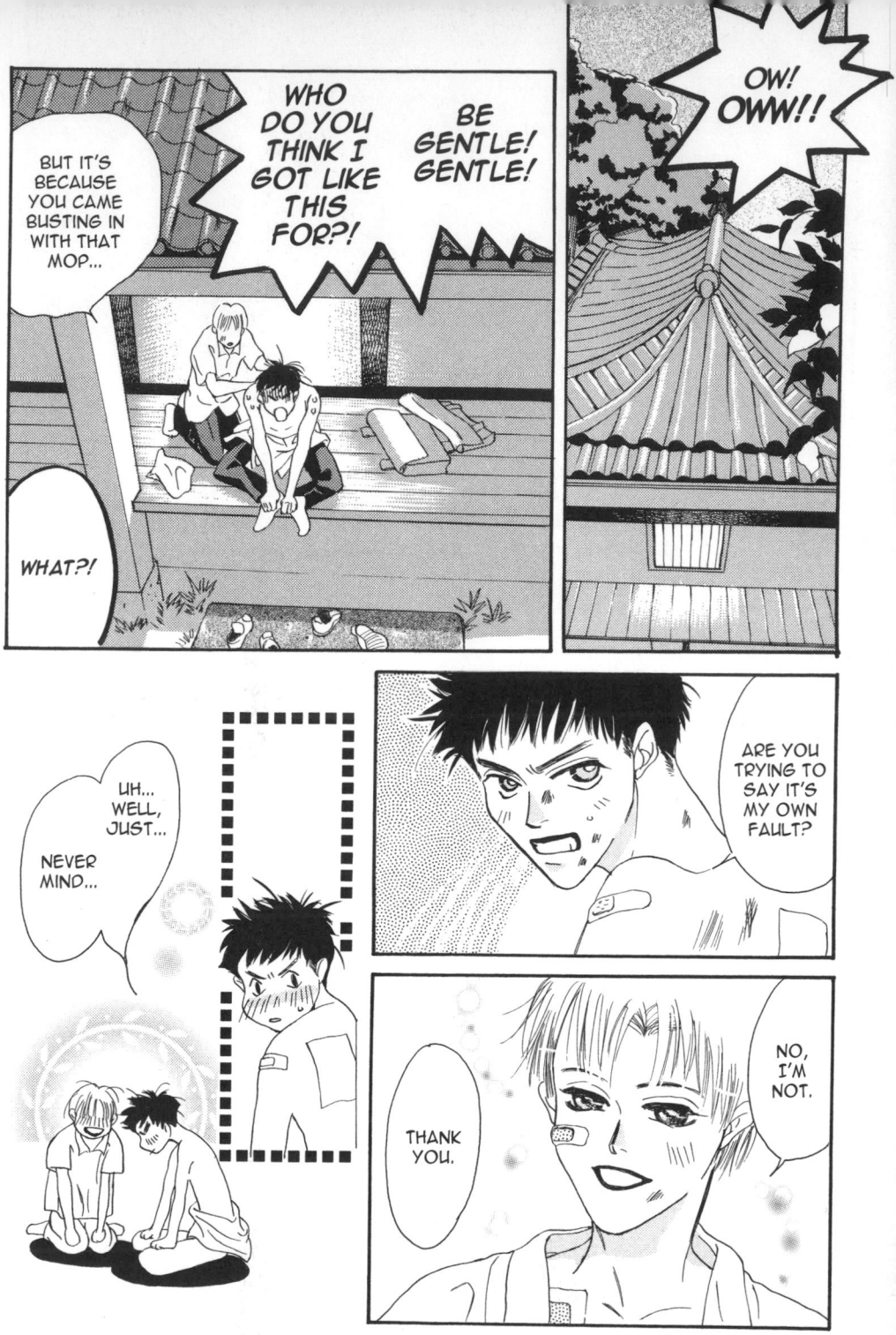
BUT IT'S BECAUSE YOU CAME BUSTING IN WITH THAT MOP...
WHO DO YOU THINK I GOT LIKE THIS FOR?!
BE GENTLE! GENTLE!
WHAT?!
OW! OWW!!
ARE YOU TRYING TO SAY IT'S MY OWN FAULT?
UH... WELL, JUST...
NEVER MIND...
NO, I'M NOT.
THANK YOU.

SAYA!
—YA!!
—OM!!
MR. HANAMORI.
MR. TSURUGI.
THERE YOU ARE, YOU LITTLE RUNTS!
I'M SORRY...
BROTHER ...
IF YOU'RE GOING TO BE LATE, AT LEAST GIVE US A CALL!
YOU FOOL!

I'M SO GLAD ...
HUG
YOU FOOL...
PUFF
PUFF
HUFF
HUFF
I'VE NEVER BEEN YELLED AT BY YOU BEFORE.

UHH...
IT SEEMS BAKA-OMI DIDN'T WANT ANYONE TO SEE HIS WOUNDS...
OR PUT UP A TANTRUM.
SORRY.
THANKS, HANAMORI.

HOP
HOP

IF THERE HAD BEEN SOMEONE LIKE MASAOMI AT HIS OTHER SCHOOL...
SAYA MIGHT NOT HAVE HAD TO CHANGE SCHOOLS...
...THE WAY HE DID.

WHO SAID...
...YOU COULD CALL ME TSURUGI?

TSURUGI.

OR, PERHAPS IT'S THANKS TO YOU?

URK!
OH, NO! MY INNER VOICE...!

AND YET, SOMEHOW, I HAD A FEELING IT WOULD TURN OUT THIS WAY...
...WOULD BE TALKING TO YOU LIKE THIS.
I DIDN'T BELIEVE THAT I...
AT THE SPRING FINALS...

...SINCE THAT TIME YOU STOPPED ME IN THE STREET.
YAEGASHI...
THAT YOU?
WHAT IF...
YOU'RE A NICER GUY THAN I THOUGHT YOU WERE...
I'M DISAP-POINTED.
WHAT IF I...
..LOVED HIM SO MUCH THAT I COULDN'T STAND IT...

WHAT IF...
WHOOSH

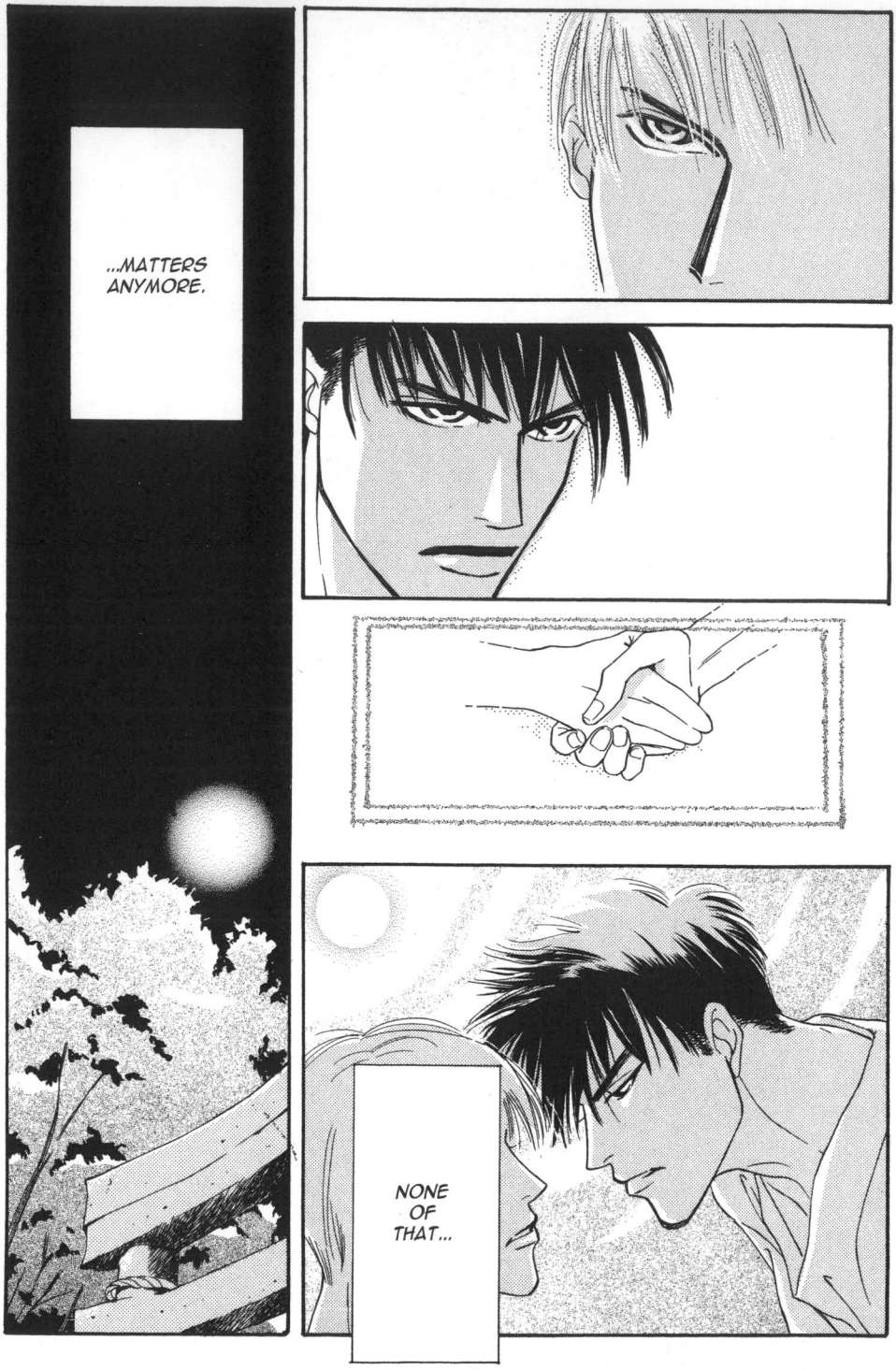
...MATTERS ANYMORE.
NONE OF THAT...

HEEEY, BRO!

YOU'RE BOTH RED.
HUH?
A-ARE WE?

OH, FINALLY!
WHAT WERE YOU GUYS DOING?

AREN'T YOU GONNA SCOLD ME TOO?
TO GIVE YOU A CALL?
NO, I'M NOT.
YOU DID GOOD.

HEEY, BRO—

'SHAY!
EHHHN!!
花森(勝)
HANAMORI (KATSU)
八重樫(剣)
YAEGASHI (TSURUGI)
HANA-MORI.

THINGS ARE GOING SMOOTHLY.
YEAH.
YO.

COMPARED TO YOUR LOG-SPLITTING BLOWS,
HE'S NOTHING!
HA HA HA!
FINE, I KNOW. EXCUSE ME FOR BEING A STAMPEDING-BOAR WARRIOR.

ONE POINT!
RED!

BOW!
NANAMI OF KYOBASHI WON.
HE'S TOUGH.

YEAH, WE ARE.
LOOKS LIKE WE'RE GOING TO MEET IN THE FINALS.
STANDING HERE NOW, I KNOW.
LATER.
SEE YOU LATER.
I'M UP AGAINST NANAMI NEXT.

EVEN IF MY LOVE FOR TSURUGI IS OVER-WHELMING...
EVEN IF TSURUGI LOVES ME BACK...

KAZE KITARU - THE WIND COMETH • END

緑深し
AO FUKASHI-DEEP GREEN
CLAK CLAK
ファーン
VROOOM
TSURUGI!
SO, WE'RE ON THE SAME TRAIN!
YOU'RE A HEAD TALLER THAN EVERY-ONE ELSE...
I SPOTTED YOU IMME-DIATELY.
CLAK CLAK CLAK
THREE GRILLED BEEF BOX LUNCHES AND TWO TEAS.
HANA-MORI!

緑深し
AO FUKAISHI ~ DEEP GREEN
あおふかし

CLAK
CLAK
CLAK
WE'RE GOING INTO TRAINING TO PREPARE FOR THE NATIONAL TOURNAMENT.
A MASS PILGRIMAGE OF SEVENTY PEOPLE.
AH.
THAT'S RIGHT... SHINAGAWA PRIVATE HIGH GOT THE TEAM WIN AT THE CITY TOURNAMENT.
GETTING TO IWATE A WHOLE WEEK EARLY...
I THOUGHT I WOULD BE THE ONLY ONE.
SORRY, HANAMORI.
YOU WANTED TO BE THE FIRST ON THE SCENE, DIDN'T YOU?
WHAT AM I, A LITTLE KID?
HA HA HA ...
CLAK
CLAK
OUR TEMP COACH HAS THIS HOBBY— HE'S A FOLK STORY RESEARCH NUT.
TEMP COACH?
HE INSISTED ON GOING OUT TO TOHNO...
AND I WAS FORCED TO ACCOMPANY HIM, THAT'S ALL!

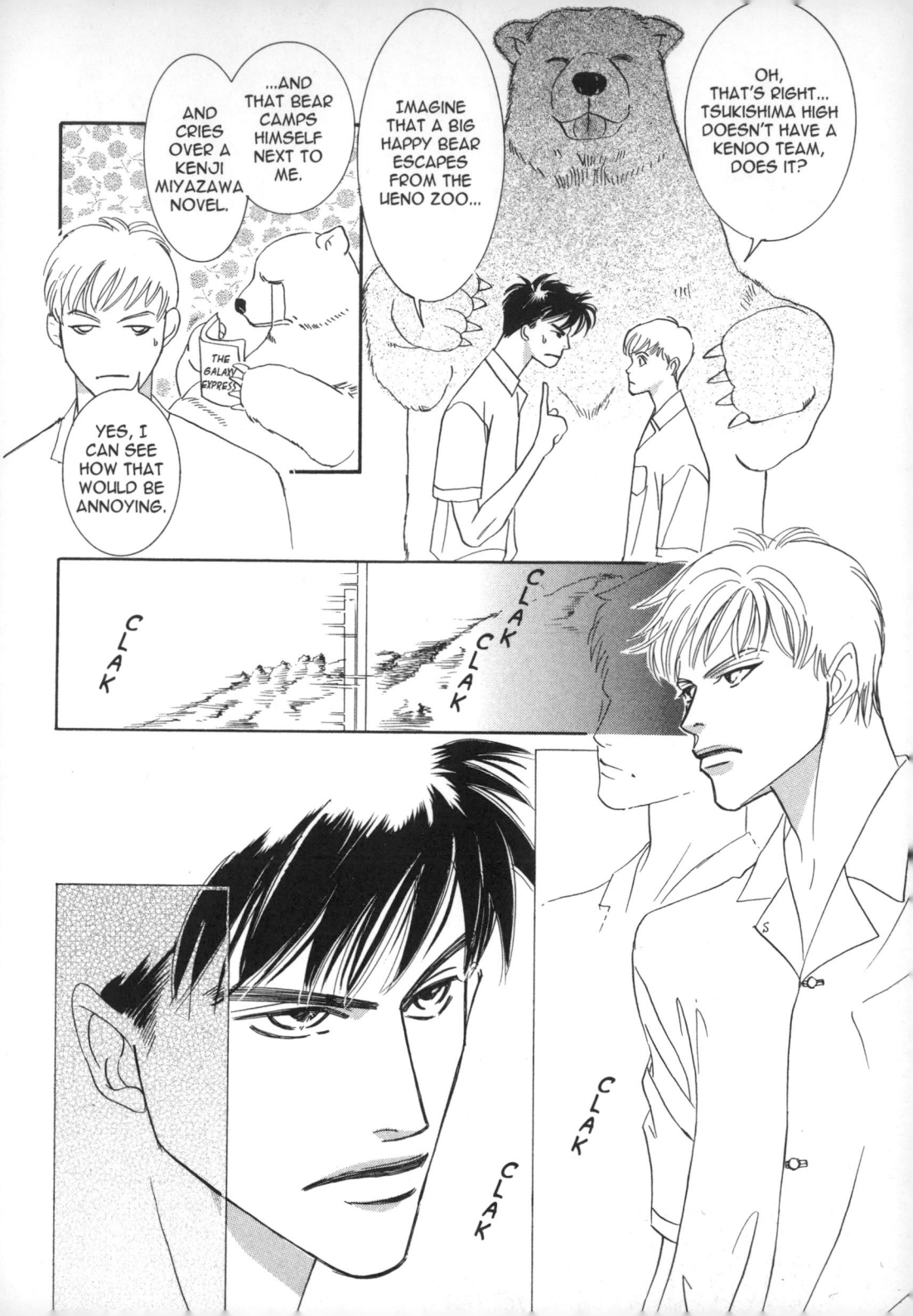
AND CRIES OVER A KENJI MIYAZAWA NOVEL.
...AND THAT BEAR CAMPS HIMSELF NEXT TO ME.
THE GALAXY EXPRESS
YES, I CAN SEE HOW THAT WOULD BE ANNOYING.
IMAGINE THAT A BIG HAPPY BEAR ESCAPES FROM THE UENO ZOO...
OH, THAT'S RIGHT... TSUKISHIMA HIGH DOESN'T HAVE A KENDO TEAM, DOES IT?
CLAK
CLAK
CLAK
CLAK
CLAK
CLAK

IT'S ONLY BEEN TWO MONTHS SINCE I BRUSHED HIS LIPS WITH MINE...
...BUT I'M ALREADY LOSING MYSELF...
I NEVER THOUGHT WE'D BE ON THE SAME TRAIN.
TO BE HONEST, I HESITATED TO EVEN COME TALK TO YOU.
WITH THE NATIONAL TOURNA-MENT APPROACH-ING...
IT'S HARD FOR ME TO EVEN BE STANDING NEXT TO YOU.
THIS SUFFOCATING FEELING...

CLAK
TSURUGI ...
TSURUGI!
CLAK
TINGLING FINGERTIPS...
WHAT IS THIS FEELING?
GULP
I WONDER IF HE'D BE MAD IF I KISSED HIM HERE...
HANA-MORI.
THIS IS OUR TEAM LEADER, MOROOKA.
じろ
GLARE
MOROOKA, THIS IS KATSUOMI HANAMORI.
ばちっ
SPARK
YOU KNOW HIM. HE WON THE INDIVIDUAL TOURNAMENT CATEGORY AT THE CITY FINALS.
WHAT ARE YOU DOING? WE'RE ABOUT TO BEGIN THE MEETING.
MOROOKA.

THIS IS WHERE WE'RE STAYING.
GIVE ME A CALL.
I THOUGHT WE'D ASK SOME ELEMENTARY SCHOOL NEARBY OR SOMETHING...
HUH? OH.
HANAMORI, WHERE ARE YOU HAVING YOUR FIELD PRACTICE?
FORGET THE INTRODUCTIONS! HURRY UP!
IT'S BETTER TO PRACTICE WITH AN OPPONENT, ISN'T IT?
TSURUGI!
I'LL ASK MY COACH IF WE CAN HAVE A JOINT PRACTICE SESSION.
A PRIVATE CAR...
I HATE DISTINGUISHED SCHOOLS...
...
...
THE NUMBER NINE CAR, FIRST FLOOR!
WAIT, TSURUGI! WHAT SEAT ARE YOU IN?!

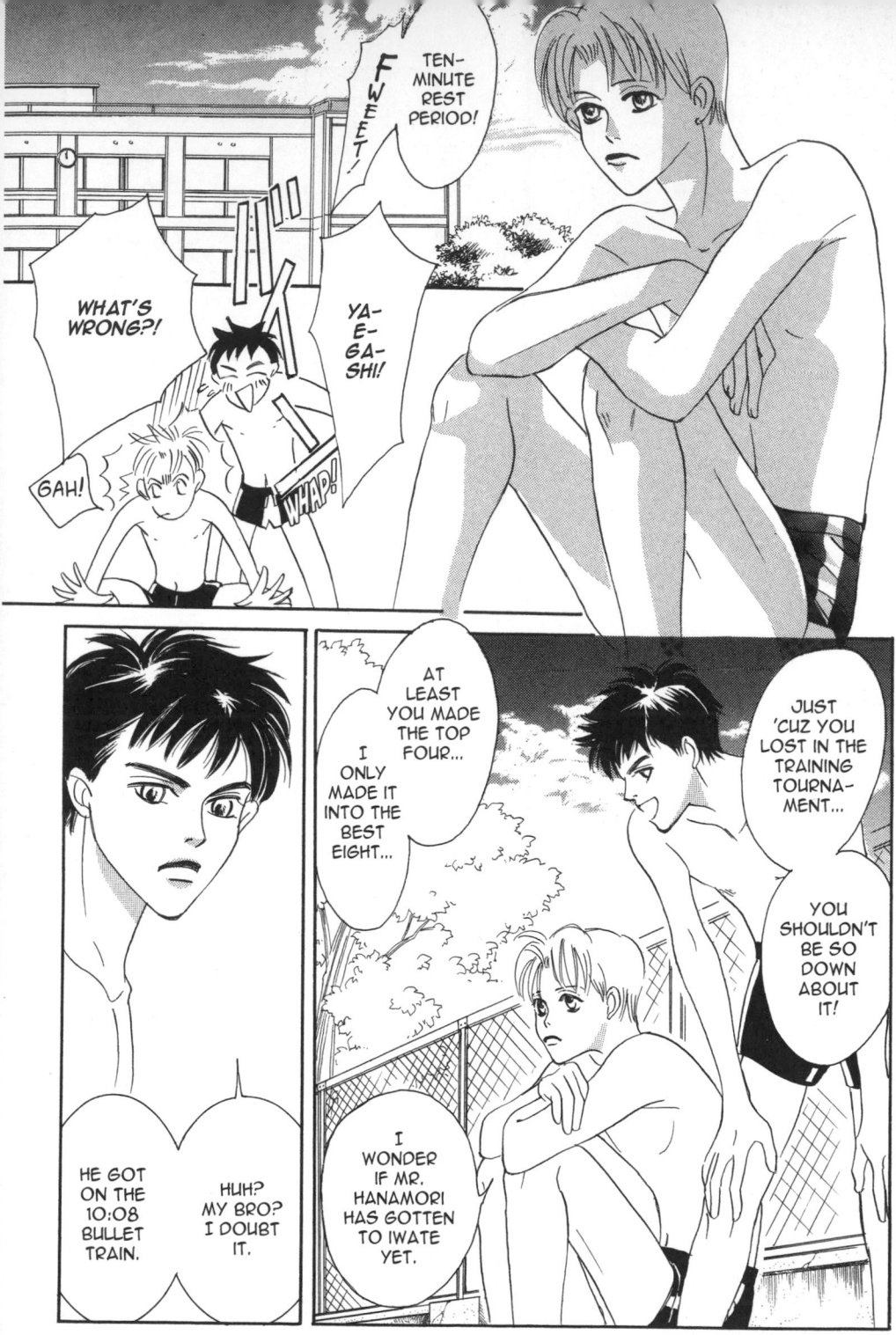
TEN-MINUTE REST PERIOD!
FWEET!
YA-E-GA-SHI!
WHAT'S WRONG?!
GAH!
WHAP!
JUST 'CUZ YOU LOST IN THE TRAINING TOURNA-MENT...
YOU SHOULDN'T BE SO DOWN ABOUT IT!
AT LEAST YOU MADE THE TOP FOUR...
I ONLY MADE IT INTO THE BEST EIGHT...
I WONDER IF MR. HANAMORI HAS GOTTEN TO IWATE YET.
HE GOT ON THE 10:08 BULLET TRAIN.
HUH? MY BRO? I DOUBT IT.

THAT'S THE SAME TRAIN AS MY BROTHER!
REALLY? WITH MR. TSURUGI?
THEN THEY'VE PROBABLY MET UP ON-BOARD.
NO WAY!
YOU DON'T HAVE TO YELL.
THOSE TWO ARE RIVALS!
THEY'RE REPRESENTATIVES FROM THE SAME AREA, SO THEY PROBABLY WON'T BE IN THE SAME INDIVIDUAL TOURNAMENT BLOCK!
I BET THEY WON'T EVEN TALK TO EACH OTHER!
YOU THINK ...?
I DON'T THINK MY BRO OR MR. TSURUGI ARE BOTHERED BY ANY OF THAT, THOUGH.
1
2
3
4
5
6

*NOTE: PORTABLE SHRINE.
HEY, NEVER MIND THAT.
IN AUGUST, DURING THE OBON, OUR TOWN'S HAVING A FESTIVAL.
A GROUP OF GUYS RUN UP THE SHRINE STEPS, HAULING THE FIGHTING MIKOSHI.*
AND THERE'LL BE FIREWORKS OVER HARUMI.
WHY DON'T YOU COME ALONG?
THE GUYS FROM CLASS WILL BE THERE—GIRLS, TOO.
IS MR. HANAMORI GOING?
WHY DO YOU KEEP ASKING ABOUT MY BRO...?
WHAT'S HE GOT TO DO WITH IT...
REST PERIOD OVER!
FWEET!
IF HE'S ALL YOU CAN TALK ABOUT, WHY DON'T YOU GO WITH HIM THEN?!
OKAY, I'LL DO THAT.

I'M JUST KIDDING! I'LL INVITE BRO ALONG...
SO LET'S GO TOGETH-ER!
OKAY!
I'LL CALL YOU LATER, THEN!
HOW CUTE ...
HE'S CHEERED UP ALREADY ...
... DAMMIT.
SO WHAT? SO WHAT?
WHAT'S WITH HIM ANYWAY? DAMN...
ANAMORI, STOP LACKING OFF!! WEET!

IWATE
NUMBER 5
岩手第五小
YAAAHH!!
WHAP
WHAP
EEEK!
STUNNED
WHAP

HANAMORI HAS GOOD SWORD HANDLING.
HIS MOVEMENTS ARE NATURAL AND THERE'S NO HESITATION BUT HE IS A STAMPEDING-BOAR WARRIOR.
HIS TYPE MAY BE WEAK DURING CLOSE COMBAT.
MOROOKA.
THIS JOINT PRACTICE WAS A GOOD IDEA.
IT SHOULD LIGHT A FIRE UNDER SOME OF OUR GUYS.
COACH ...
YES.
TAKE HIM ON.

HE NEVER LOSES HIS MA-AI.*
*NOTE: PROPER DISTANCE
HE'S GOTTEN MUCH STRONGER SINCE THE CITY TOURNAMENT.

YOUR STRENGTH EXCITES ME.
THIS FEELING...
SMACK
IT RESEMBLES SOMETHING ELSE.
BAM

WE'LL HAVE A THIRTY MINUTE REST PERIOD.
OK! THAT'S ENOUGH.
AN OTOSHI-MEN*... YOU WERE TOO EAGER FOR THE WIN, MOROOKA.
*NOTE: COUNTERSTRIKE TO HELMET...
HANAMORI IS DEFINITELY STRONG.

MATCH WON!
BAM
DID YOU WIN AGAIN, HANAMORI?
OH, MAN...
HUFF HUFF PANT PANT
ゆあっ
Ohhh
SOUNDS LIKE THERE WAS AN UPSET ON THE OTHER COURT.
BEAR... THAT'S COLD...
WHEEZE
HUFF
PANT
JUST LOSE ALREADY.
I WANT TO GO VISIT THE STORY-TELLER'S HOUSE TODAY.

みーん
ZEEEEK
みんみん
ZEKZEEK
みーん
ZEEEEK
みーん
ZEEEEK
みんみん
ZEKZEEK
みーん
ZEEEEK
A - BLOCK
SEMI-FINALS
HANAMORI, KATSUOMI (TSU
KIMURA, MAKOTO (HAKO
HANAMORI, KATSUOMI
FINALS
YAEGASHI

SO, YOU WERE LISTENING... THAT'S NOT FAIR.
ONLY PEOPLE WHO ARE SURE OF THEIR SUPERIORITY CAN HOLD HIS KIND OF PHILOSOPHY.
HE SURE MUST HAVE CONFIDENCE IN HIMSELF
FOR HERE. EVERYONE.
ゴトン
CLUNK
WHEN YOU'RE STRONG...
I'M EVEN HAPPIER.

ZEEEK
ZEEEK
ZEEEK
SO, YOU LIKE A STRONG MAN, TSURUGI?
ZEEK
ZIKZIK
WHAT ARE YOU TALKING ABOUT, LEADER?
ZEEK
ENOUGH TO INVITE HIM TO JOINT PRAC-TICE?
I'M STRIVING TO MAKE MYSELF STRONGER.
THAT WON'T HAPPEN IF MY OPPO-NENT IS WEAK.
WHEN HE'S STRONG, IT MAKES ME HAPPY.
THAT'S WHY I INVITED HIM TO PRACTICE.
THAT'S ALL.
IN A MATCH, THE RESULT IS ALL THAT MATTERS.
YOU'RE SOFT, TSURUGI.

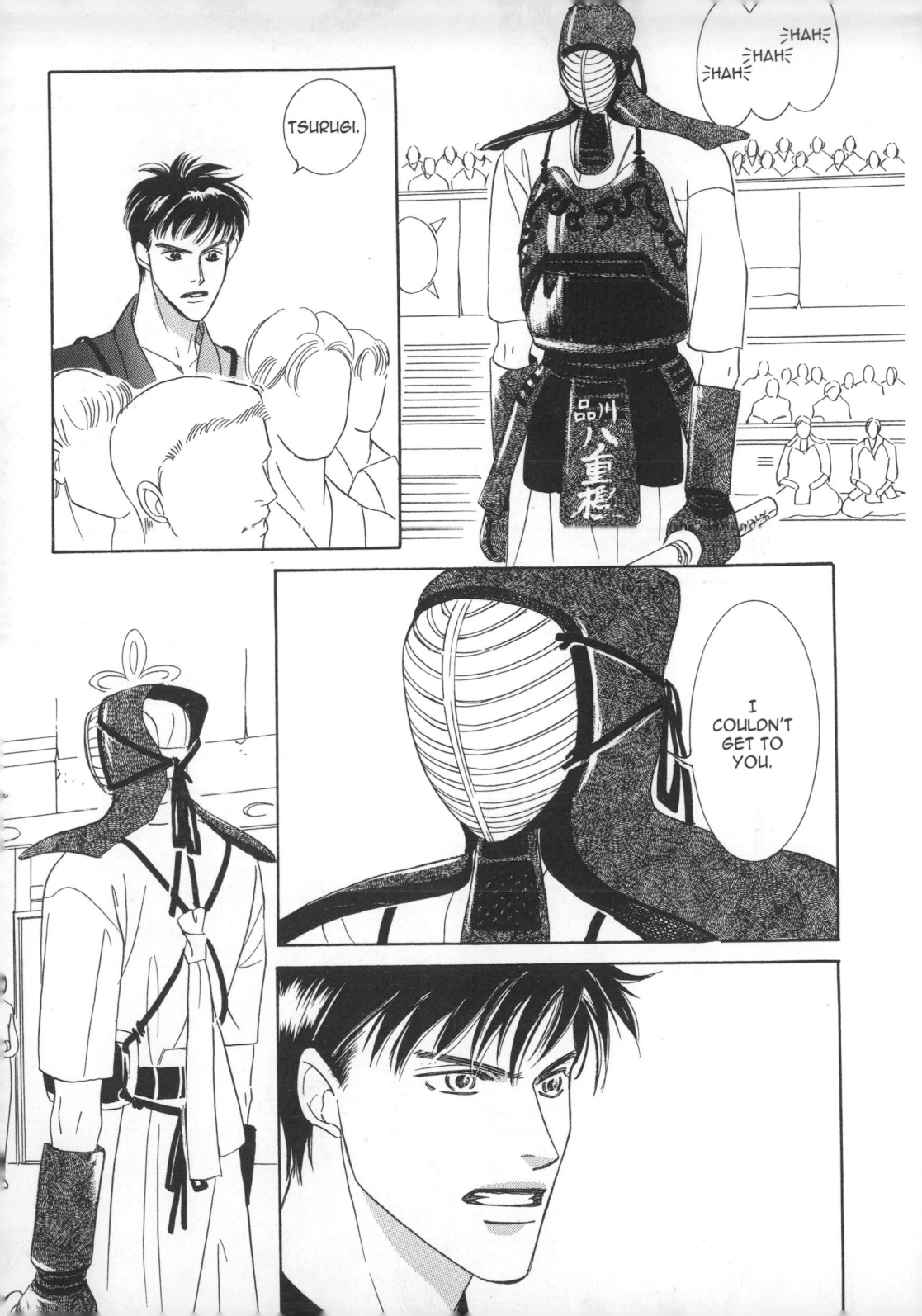
TSURUGI.
HAH
HAH
HAH
品川
八重樫
I COULDN'T GET TO YOU.

HANAMORI, KATSUOMI 2 (3)
(TSUKISHIMA MUNICIPAL HIGH)
HANA MORI, KAT-SUOMI
(TSUKI-SHIMA MUNI-CIPAL
FINALS
INAN, TET-SUYUKI
(KUMA-MOTO PRE-FEC-TURAL
YAEGASHI, TSURUGI 2 (3)
(SHINAGAWA PRIVATE HIGH)
THE NATIONAL HIGH SCHOOL KENDO TOURNA-MENT...
FINALS MATCH WILL NOW BEGIN.
ONE MORE.
月島
花森

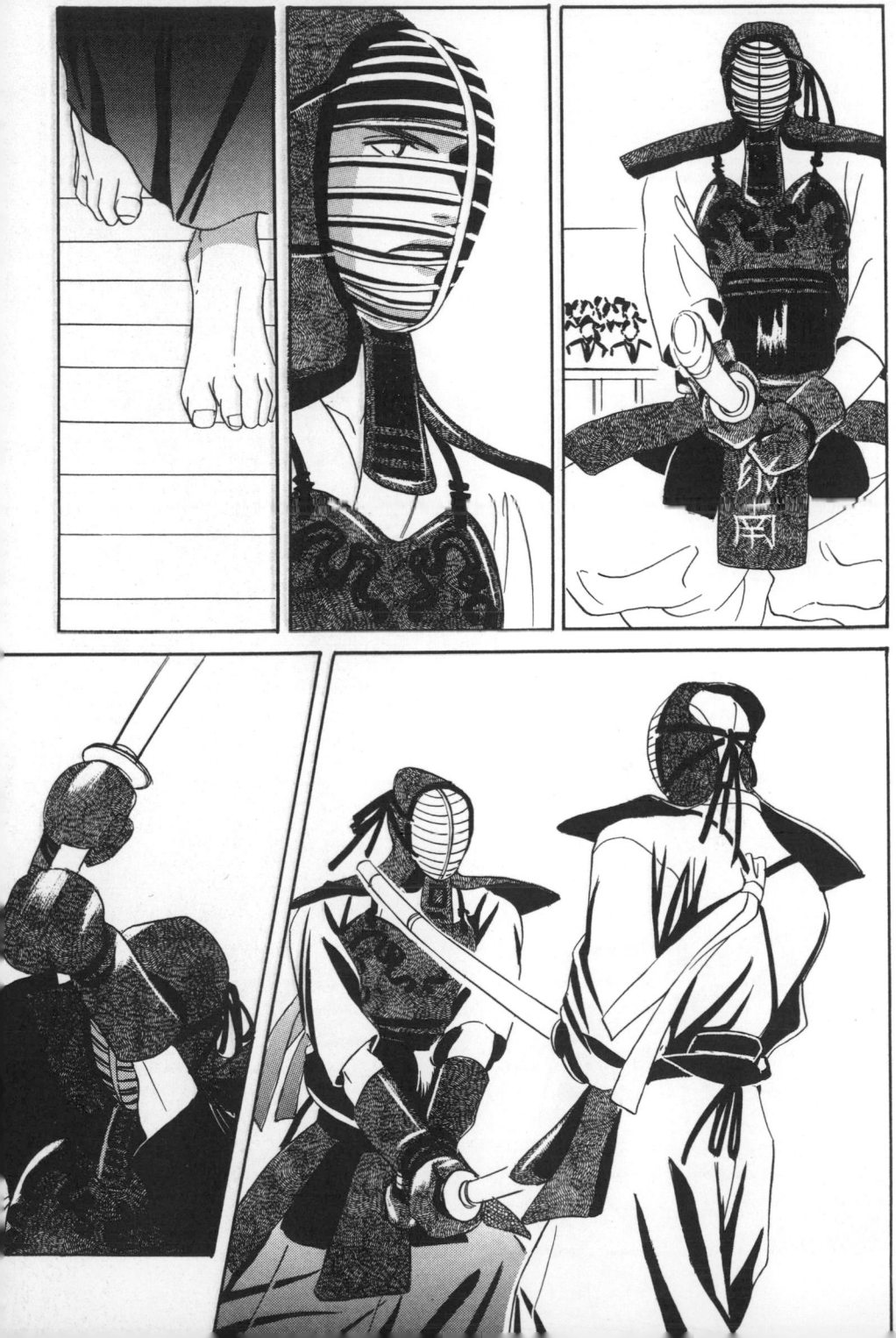

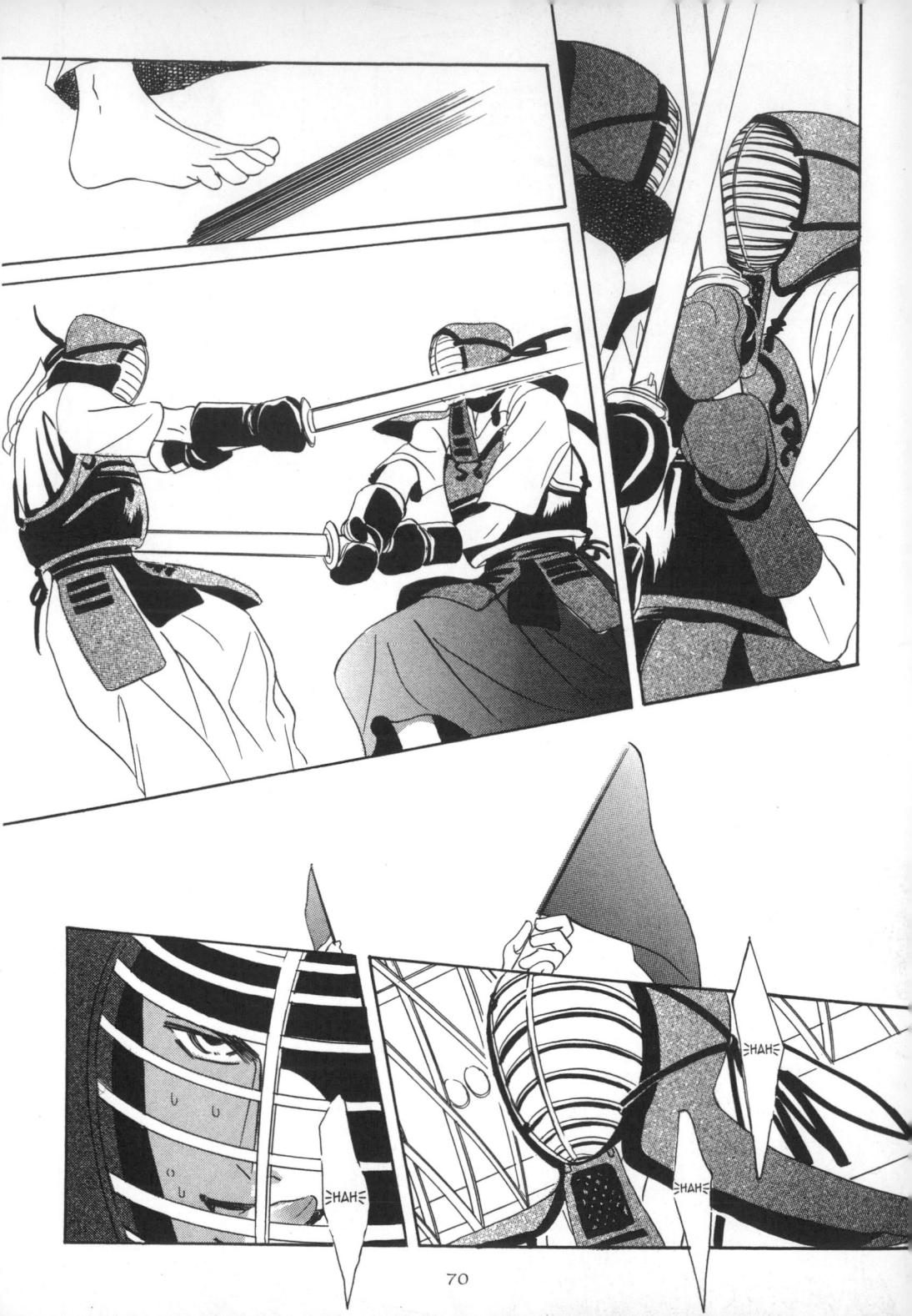
HAH
HAH
HAH

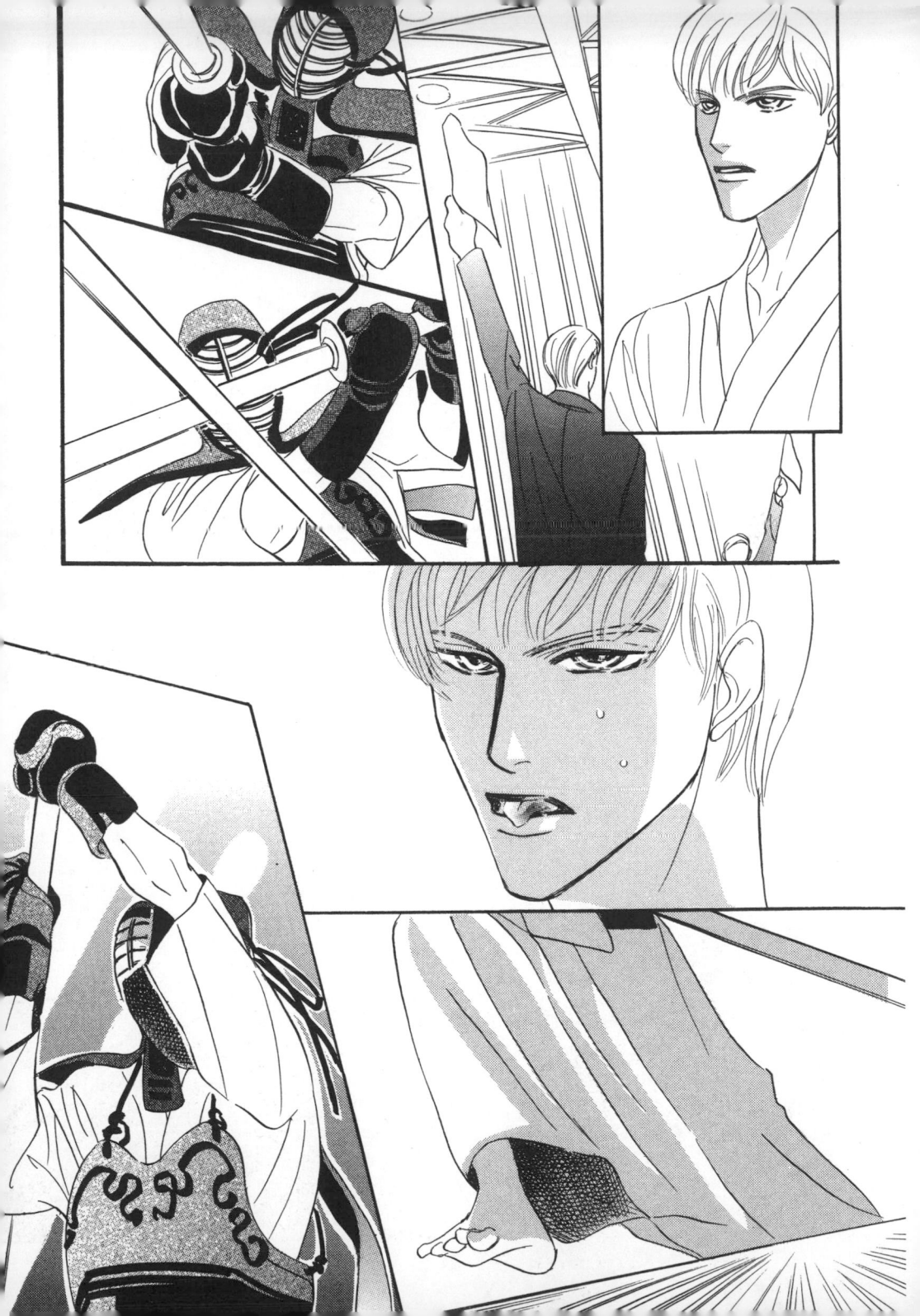

HE WON?
TSURUGI.

TEAM TOURNAMENT RESULTS
WINNER: SHINAGAWA PRIVATE HIGH
2ND PLACE: OOITA NUMBER ONE HIGH
3RD PLACE: SEIRYO PRIVATE HIGH
OUTSTANDING INDIVIDUALS
TADANORI MOROOKA (SHINAGAWA PRIVATE
TSURUGI YAEGASHI (SHINAGAWA PRIVATE

ドン
BOOM
WHAT IS IT, MASAOMI?
I'M ABOUT TO GO CARRY THE MIKOSHI.
NEVER-MIND THAT!
YOU CAN ALWAYS CARRY THE MIKOSHI NEXT YEAR!
BUT YOU'RE ONLY YOUNG ONCE!
I'M IN FRONT THIS YEAR...
パチパチパチ
CRACKLE
CRACKLE
CRACKLE
TACHISI CORP.
HANA-MORI FISH SHOP
MIYAMA LIQUOR STORE
TOKYO ROAD-STING
BRO!
OVER HERE!

MR. HANA-MORI.
HEY.
SPARK
ぱんっ
SO, THAT'S *THAT*— YOU'RE GONNA HAVE TO ACCOMPANY US THIS YEAR, BRO!

WHAT ABOUT YOU, SAYA?
SST
HUH? ME TOO?
AND YOU CAN TAKE YOUR PICK OF PRIZES. WHAT DO YOU WANT?
ONE MORE OF THOSE BOXES...
I WANT A GIANTS CARD!
OOH!
HERE, MASA. YOU GET THE LAST ONE.
TOSS
HUH?! WHA?!
BRO!
TSURUGI!
TSURUGI.

BOOM
ドドドン
BABOOM
BABOOM
BOOM
BOOM
BOOM
BOOM
ドドドン
BABOOM
ドドドン
BOOM

UH...
I CAN'T STOP MYSELF.
WHAT TO DO...
AT THE NATIONAL TOURNAMENT...

HAH
HUFF
HAH
HUFF

OF COURSE. YOU'RE SHARPER THAN I THOUGHT.
THEY'RE KIDS.
IT'S JUST PUBERTY.
HE'LL SOON FORGET SUCH FEELINGS.
BUT EVEN IF THAT'S NOT THE CASE...
THERE'S NOTHING I CAN DO FOR HIM.

SAYA SEEMS TO HOLD...
...SPECIAL FEELINGS FOR YOU.
I KNOW.

...I MEANT TO REACH THE FINALS.
I MEANT TO CROSS SWORDS WITH YOU.
I HAD THE CONFIDENCE TO WIN AGAINST YOU.
I'M RESENT-FUL.
I FEEL AS IF I'M GOING TO LOSE TO YOU IN EVERYTHING.
IT SICKENS ME.

カラン CLAK
THIS IS THE ULTIMATE CONFESSION...
...BUT ALSO A CRUEL REJECTION.
カラン CLAK
カラン CLAK
カラン CLAK
カラン CLAK

THEN BRING IT ON, TSURUGI.
I'LL WIN AGAINST YOU AS MANY TIMES AS IT TAKES.
YOU'LL SEE.
I'LL MAKE YOU SUBMIT BY FORCE.
CRACKLE CRACKLE CRACKLE
パラパラパラ
ドオン
BOOM

AO FUKASHI - DEEP GREEN / END

AND YET, HE SOMEHOW STILL MANAGES TO GET INTO MEDICAL SCHOOL... AMAZING.
NEXT! ANYONE!
YES! I - HANAMORI!
PLEASE GO ONE ROUND WITH ME, MR. TSURUGI!
きゅう
K.O.

TSUKISHIMA KENDOJO
月島剣道場
BAM
NEXT!
BAM
NEXT!
EVEN DURING THE TIME OFF FOR COLLEGE ENTRANCE EXAMS, I HEARD HE WAS PRACTICING ON HIS OWN.
THAT SUMMER TOURNAMENT LAST YEAR MUST'VE REALLY GOT TO HIM.
TSURUGI SEEMS REALLY DRIVEN!

道ゆかば
MICHI YUKABA-
DOWN THIS ROAD

ON THE NIGHT OF THE SUMMER FESTIVAL, WE SAW A MIRAGE.
THE FIREWORKS REFLECTED BEAUTIFULLY ON THE RIVER'S SURFACE...
MICHI YUKABA- DOWN THIS ROAD

EVERYONE - SIT!
I-I'M OKAY...
BLUSH
UH...
ARE YOU ALL RIGHT, MASAOMI?
IT'S MY FIRST FREE PRACTICE IN A WHILE... I GOT A LITTLE OVER-EXCITED.
I MAKE MY FIRST VISIT TO THE DOJO IN A WHILE, AND WHAT DO I FIND...
YOU ALL SEEM TO HAVE SLACKED OFF AT THE START OF A NEW SCHOOL SEMESTER.
I SUSPECT THAT YOU'RE USING THE MASTER'S ABSENCE DUE TO ILLNESS AS AN EXCUSE TO SHIRK PRACTICE.
BEG PARDON ...

SST...
PUT MORE STRENGTH INTO YOUR GUT, SAYA.
YOU DO IT, KATSUOMI.
DUM- ドタドタ DUM
DUM ドタドタ
DUM-
CUT IT OUT!
I HAVE COME TO TAKE YOUR DOJO SIGN!
KATSUOMI HANAMORI, DOJO-BUSTER, ANNOUNCES HIS ARRIVAL!
IT'S EMBARRASSING! STUPID BRO!
HUFF
HUFF

I HEARD THAT HE WAS ILL...
IS MASTER OHMORI HERE?
BAKA-OMI.
HE STRAINED HIS BACK. THIS WAY, PLEASE.
HEY! IT'S MINATO DOJO'S HANAMORI NIDAN! HE'S SO COOL... I WONDER WHAT HE'S DOING AT OUR DOJO?
WHO'S THE LITTLE GUY?
THAT MUST BE MR. TSURUGI'S LITTLE BROTHER, SAYA. HE'S GOOD. LIKE A SAMURAI AND HIS SQUIRE.

YEAH.
OHHH
YO, LONG-TIME, NO-SEE.
HMM.
MASTER HONUMA, CAN I JUST...
SAYA, HURRY UP.
WANNA?
OK.

OOHHH, UONUMA... THANKS FOR COMING ALL THE WAY OVER.
IT'S ALL RIGHT - JUST STAY DOWN.
YOU MEAN WE CAN GO TO SUMMER TRAINING CAMP WITH MINATO DOJO?!
I'M AGAINST IT.
I CAN'T TEACH IN THIS CONDITION...
TSURUGI YAEGASHI IS OUR HIGHEST RANKING STUDENT, BUT HE'S A MED STUDENT...I CAN'T IMPOSE ON HIM TO TAKE CHARGE ALL THE TIME.
WELL, WE CAN JOIN UP OUR DOJOS FOR THE SUMMER TRAINING CAMP SESSION...
AND I CAN SEND DOWN AKITA FROM OUR DOJO FOR REGULAR PRACTICE...
WHAT ?!
WHY?
HAVE YOU FORGOTTEN, HANAMORI?
THE NIGHT OF THE SUMMER FESTIVAL...

MASTER! PLEASE COME RIGHT AWAY!
...OH.
THE FESTI-VAL...
MR. TSURUGI ...
SHAH
SHAH
SHAH
SHAH
SHAH
MR. HANAMORI IS...!
MR. HANA-MORI!
SOMEONE CALL AN AMBULANCE!

MASTER HONUMA ...
DASH
YOU FOOL! WHAT DO YOU THINK YOU'RE DOING!
MASTER.
I'M SORRY.
I'M THE ONE WHO CONTINUED ATTACKING HANAMORI EVEN THOUGH HE WAS OUT-OF-BOUNDS.

ARE YOU ALL RIGHT, HANAMORI?
IT'S NOTHING.
ON THE NIGHT OF THE SUMMER FESTIVAL, WE SAW A MIRAGE.
DOES MY BROTHER LOVE THAT BEAUTIFUL PERSON?
AND THAT BEAUTIFUL PERSON...

LOOKING GOOD, HANAMORI.
NOT LIKELY.
...DOES HE HATE MY BROTHER?
YEAH.
DOJO GRADUATE.
I THINK HE'S THE ONE THAT'S SUFFERING MORE SERIOUSLY. IT'S NOT LIKE TSURUGI TO LOSE HIS COOL.
WHAT HAPPENED? ANY IDEA?
THERE'S NO GLASS LEFT IN THE WOUND, AND IT'S NOT DEEP ENOUGH FOR STITCHES.
BE SURE TO DISINFECT AND CHANGE THE GAUZE DAILY.

THE PROBLEM IS WHAT TO DO ABOUT IT...
I'M RESENTFUL.
EVER SINCE YOUR REJECTION THE NIGHT OF THE SUMMER FESTIVAL, I'VE THOUGHT ABOUT IT.
I HAD THE CONFIDENCE TO WIN AGAINST YOU. BUT NOW...
I CAN'T JUST PRETEND IT NEVER HAPPENED.
TSURUGI—
TSUKISHIMA MUNICIPAL JUNIOR HIGH SCHOOL
I FEEL AS IF I'M GOING TO LOSE TO YOU IN EVERYTHING.
I'M RESENTFUL...

HANAMORI FISH SHOP
IT'S BECAUSE OF YOU GUYS, YOU KNOW.
I SEE. SO YOU ANGERED "PRINCESS" SAYA.
HURRY AND MAKE-UP. IT'S POISONING THE ATMOSPHERE.
YOU AND MR. TSURUGI ARE LIKE THE FACES OF OUR RESPECTIVE DOJOS.
SORRY I'M LATE, HANAMORI.

KOJIMA! SHUT UP, YOU!
NYAAH.
FYI, WE'RE ALL SUPPOSED TO MEET AT MINATO DOJO TODAY.
HA HA— HANAMORI GOT DUMPED BY SAYA!
...I MADE HIM MAD...
YOU'LL DIE OF ASPHYXIA-TION.
YOU'RE WRONG. BIG BROTHER HANAMORI AND MR. TSURUGI ETERNALLY EMIT A FLORAL BOUQUET SCENT!
WHATEVER.
YEAH, KEEP DREAMING! BRO HAS REALLY STINKY FEET, YOU KNOW.
I GET TO SEE BIG BROTHER HANAMORI— YAAAY!

I SUPPORT THE JOINT TRAINING CAMP IDEA.
OUR TSUKISHIMA DOJO IS LUCKY TO HAVE MASTER HONUMA TEACHING US.
I'M NOT SURE I AGREE WITH YOU.
YOU'RE LUCKY, MASAOMI. YOU DON'T CARE AS LONG AS YOU GET TO BE WITH MY BIG BROTHER.
WHAT DO I CARE?!
WE'RE NOT IN THE SAME CLASS ANYMORE, SO WE WON'T BE SEEING EACH OTHER AS OFTEN.
LET'S NOT PART IN A FIGHT.
OH, I'LL BE LATE FOR THE STUDENT COUNCIL INAUGURAL CEREMONY.
WHAT'S THAT MEAN? IT'S YOU THAT I WANT TO...

YEAH, I'M REALLY LOOKING FORWARD TO IT.
IT'S NOT THAT...
THANKS...
AND ABOUT THE JOINT TRAINING CAMP...
I JUST DON'T THINK WE SHOULD HAVE JOINT EXERCISES RIGHT NOW.
THERE WAS TROUBLE THAT OTHER TIME... REMEMBER? IF SOMETHING LIKE THAT HAPPENED AGAIN AT TRAINING CAMP...
AND I WANTED TO ASK YOU FOR YOUR HELP...
WWW- WHAT ARE YOU SAYING ...?!
YOU JUST DON'T WANT TO SEE MY BRO AND MR. TSURUGI TOGETHER, RIGHT?
HMM...

MASAOMI!
I WANT TO THANK YOU.
YOU WON! CONGRATS!
NO NEED FOR THANKS.
I WAS SURPRISED WHEN YOU TOLD ME TO RUN FOR STUDENT COUNCIL, BUT...
YOU WENT THROUGH A LOT YOUR FRESHMAN YEAR.
AS LONG AS I SEE THAT YOU'RE LAUGHING AND SURROUNDED BY FRIENDS...
...THAT'S ALL THE THANKS I NEED.

AFTER THREE WEEKS OF HEATED DEBATE, THE VOTES ARE IN.
THE NEW STUDENT COUNCIL PRESIDENT IS SAYA YAEGASHI OF SECOND YEAR, CLASS A!
YEAAHH!
AYA~
ALL RIIIGHT!
GIVE HIM A ROUND OF APPLAUSE!
THAT A PERSON LIKE ME HAS BEEN HONORED WITH THIS POSITION— I OWE THIS TO MY LOYAL, RELIABLE FRIENDS.
IT IS FOR THESE FRIENDS THAT I PROMISE TO FOLLOW THROUGH WITH MY PLEDGE...
...AND WORK TOWARD ABOLISHING THE MANDATORY WEARING OF UNIFORMS, AS WELL AS CHANGING THE SCHOOL DRESS CODE.

IT'S TRUE THAT TSURUGI RESENTS ME.
WEREN'T YOU TWO FIGHTING?
HEY, HEY— BRO.
GO 'ROUND BACK TO THE BAMBOO GROVE. I'LL BE RIGHT THERE.
CAN YOU UNDER-STAND THAT, MASAOMI?
HE RESENTS ME, BUT HE LOVES ME.
FOR WHAT...?
YOU SEE, I'M WAITING.

FOR HIM TO SURRENDER TO ME...
I'M WAITING FOR HIM TO THROW AWAY HIS EGO, HIS PRIDE— EVERYTHING...
...AND FACE ME, WITH HIS HANDS UP IN THE AIR.
TAKE OVER THE SHOP FOR ME, WILL YA?
...YEAH.
I DON'T REALLY UNDER-STAND THE RELATIONSHIP BETWEEN BRO AND MR. TSURUGI.
COOL, HUH?

MICHI YUKABA - DOWN THIS ROAD / END

THE WEIGHT IS COMFORT-ABLE TO THE ARMS...
NOW I'VE SHOWN YOU EVERYTHING I'VE GOT.
IT STILLS MY SOUL...
I'M COM-PLETELY NAKED.

*NOTE: IAI IS A SWORD TECHNIQUE INVOLVING LIGHTNING-FAST SWORD REMOVAL FROM THE SCABBARD TO CUT DOWN THE OPPONENT, WITH VERY LITTLE CHANGE IN STANCE OR BODY MOVEMENT.

THIS.
WHAT IS IT YOU WANTED TO SHOW ME, HANAMORI?
BUT WHAT I DO KNOW IS THAT THEY'RE BEYOND GENDER, BEYOND VIEWPOINTS...
THEY'RE TRYING TO FORGE SOMETHING NEW TOGETHER.
...
...

君知るや
DOST THOU KNOW- PART 1

YAHOO!
WHOOAA!
SPLASH

DAAAAN
HANAMORI (ELDER)
YAEGASHI (ME)
TOTAL: 2
WARTHOG ROOM
MONKEY ROOM
THIRD YEAR JR. HIGH MALES
BOW
THANK YOU FOR YOUR TROUBLE.
THEN I'LL TAKE THIS.
WAIT, WAIT, THAT'S NOT GOOD NOT GOOD AT ALL!
TSURUGI!
WHO SAID YOU COULD CALL ME TSURUGI?
HAVE YOU BEEN LISTENING TO ME?!
US IN THE SAME ROOM... THAT'S A BAD IDEA! ESPECIALLY FOR ME!
YOU KNOW, IT'S JUST THIS SIDE OF YOU...

WHAP
MASTER UONUMA... HE'S ON A PRE-MARITAL VACATION TRIP WITH HER.

ROOM ASSIGN-MENTS.
RIGHT HERE.
FLAP

SIR KENDO STUDENTS, HAVE YOU DECIDED ON ROOM ASSIGNMENTS?
WHOAAA...I ALMOST HAD AN EXPLOSIVE NOSEBLEED JUST NOW.

ZEEEK
ZEEEK
ZEEK
ZEEK
ZEEK
ZEEK
ZEEK
ZEEK
いーんじじじじじ
HAVING TO COOK UP A TRAINING SCHEDULE AFTER ALREADY ARRIVING AT CAMP... IT'S UNPRECEDENTED.
THAT OLD FOX UONUMA... PRETENDING TO BE SICK SO HE COULD DITCH US...
SHE'S MASTER UONUMA'S GATE BALL* TEAMMATE, ISN'T SHE?
DO YOU KNOW A MISS HANAKO FROM THE MAIN STREET SHOPPING DISTRICT? THE ONE THAT WORKS IN THE CLOTHING STORE?
*NOTE: JAPANESE VERSION OF CROQUET.

- THREE DAYS BEFORE TRAINING CAMP -
MASTER OHMORI... FOR YOUR TEACHINGS THESE LONG YEARS...
I HAVE COME TO A DECISION.. AFTER THIS LAST TRAINING CAMP, I WILL BE LEAVING THE DOJO TO CONCENTRATE ON MY STUDIES.
...THANK YOU VERY MUCH.

LET'S GO GATHER UP THE LITTLE RUNTS NOW, SHALL WE?
LEAP
...THAT I FIND CUTE AND LIKEABLE.
CUTESY
BOOM
どっかーん
DAMMIT, TSURUGI... ARE YOU TRYING TO KILL ME...?
CALL ME TSURUGI YAEGASHI.

I'D FORGOTTEN—
TSURUGI YAEGASHI... HE'S LIKE THE WIND.
I MAY NEVER BE ABLE TO CATCH HIM...
IN MY LIFETIME.
CHOMP
TRY A TOMATO? IT'S SWEET.

BUT THIS IS WHAT A REAL TOMATO TASTES LIKE.
WELL, THEY PICK THE ONES THAT GO TO TOKYO WHILE THEY'RE STILL GREEN AND FORCE THEM TO RIPEN DURING SHIPMENT...
IT'S SWEET! IT'S LIKE A FRUIT...NOTHING LIKE THE ONES IN TOKYO.
USE YOUR OWN HANDS, SONNY.

DOST THOU KNOW... MY HEART...
IT'S SWEET...
DO THOU KNOWEST... THE TROPIC LAND WITHIN MY HEART...

WHAT ARE YOU DOING, SAYA?! THAT WAS TOO CLOSE!
SKOFF! SHACK!
DA-DANG!
びしっ
WHIP
ヒョオオオオオオ
WHOOOOSH
がち
CRACKLE
ん
DO THOU KNOWEST THE FROZEN LAND WITHIN MY HEART

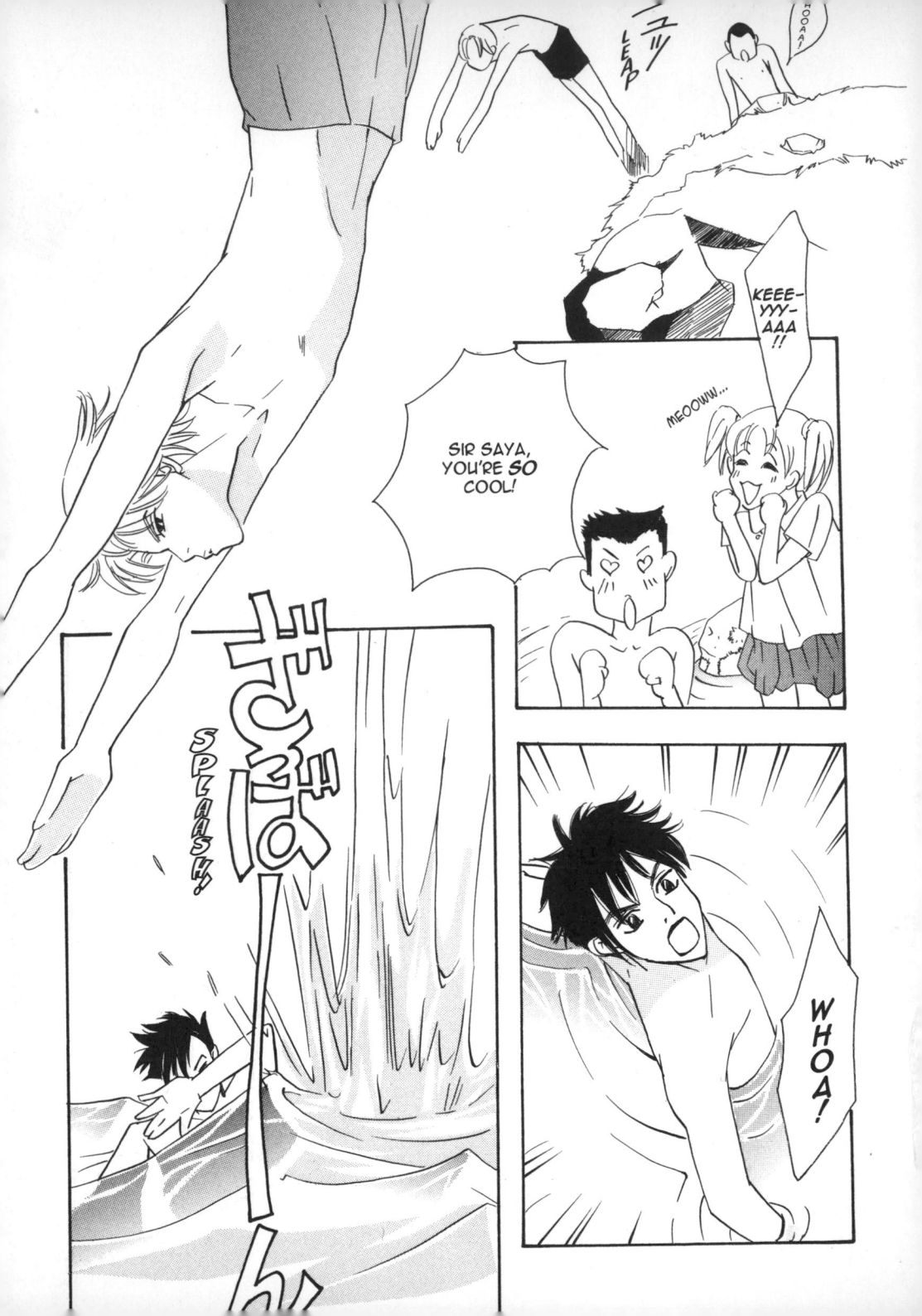
LEAP
HOOA!
KEEE-YYY-AAA!!
MEOOWW...
SIR SAYA, YOU'RE SO COOL!
WHOA!
SPLASH!

I GUESS YOU'RE RIGHT.
RIGHT ♡
OH, YOU MEAN THERE'S NOTHING BETWEEN YOU AND KOJIMA, HANAMORI? THEN MAYBE I'LL CONFESS MY LOVE TO HER DURING THIS TRAINING CAMP.
TEE HEE
GET DUMPED.
AHH, KOJIMA'S SO CUTE HER THIGHS ARE SO ATTRACTIVE...
YOU SHOULD GET YOUR EYES CHECKED, OKINO-SHIMA.
I SPY A FOUR-EYED MONKEY!

OUT!
OUT!
OUT!
OUT!
THE SENIORS WILL CHEW YOU OUT!
GUYS! THAT'S ENOUGH ALREADY!
AOI, DON'T LEAN OUT SO FAR. IT'S DANGEROUS!
I'M GOING DOWN THERE.
HEY, KOJIMA?! WHAT ARE YOU DOING?!
TUCK TUCK
SURE FEELS NICE IN HERE!
IF YOU DON'T TAKE A DIP NOW, YOU'LL REGRET IT FOR THE REST OF YOUR LIFE!
IT'S NOT FAIR THAT THE BOYS GET TO HAVE ALL THE FUN WHILE WE WATCH THE BAGS.
WE'RE WEARING BLOOMERS UNDERNEATH OUR SKIRTS ANYWAY.

ONE, TWO!
ONE, TWO!
MR. STU-DENT!
A BEAR'S HERE TO SEE YOU!
A BEAR?
ZEEK

I'M MINATO DOJO'S TEMPORARY COACH, AKITA.
ARE YOU COACH NONOHANA FROM TSUKISHIMA HIGH?
THERE'S RUMORS THAT A ZASHIKI WARASHI** SOMETIMES APPEARS IN A ROOM AT THE MINOYA.
NOW, THAT'S INTEREST-ING.
SCRIBBLE SCRIBBLE
HO-HOH! SO THE LITTLE RIVER 'ROUND BACK HAS A KAPPA* LEGEND ATTACHED TO IT.
*NOTE: A KAPPA IS A MYTHOLOGICAL WATER CREATURE, HUMAN-LIKE, BUT WITH A TURTLE SHELL ON ITS BODY.
**NOTE: A PROTECTIVE HOUSE SPIRIT.
"NONOHANA (FIELDFLOWER)"? PFFT! WHAT A CUTE NAME!
FOREIGN SPECIES INTERAC-TION.
FOLK-TALE MANIAC BEAR.
NO PROBLEM. YOU SAVED ME TRAIN FARE.
THANK YOU FOR TRAVELING SO FAR. I CAN'T HANDLE EVERY-THING HERE ALONE, SO YOU'LL BE OF GREAT HELP.

AND LIKE A LIVING THING, THE SMOKE CRAWLED ACROSS THE WALLS, SLIPPING IN THROUGH THE CRACKS OF THE STORM WINDOW.
JUST THEN, A STREAM OF WHITE SMOKE SLITHERED FROM THE GARDEN...
IT BEGAN TO AMASS ITSELF BEFORE THE MAN'S EYES.
OH, HOW STRANGE!
EEEEEEEEK!!
FRANTICALLY ROLLING LEFT AND RIGHT, IT SPOTTED THE MAN, AND...
THEN, SUDDENLY...IN THE CENTER OF THE SMOKE, A LARGE EYEBALL APPEARED...

PAFF
OH! IT'S YOU, COACH AKITA! WHAT A SCAREDY-CAT!
WAAH!
FLINCH
CLICK
HANA-MORI?
WHAT ARE YOU DOING OUT HERE ALONE?
AHA! FOUND YOUR WEAKNESS! YOU'RE SCARED OF GHOST STORIES.
GIVE IT A REST. HAVE SOME WATER-MELON.

IS THAT THE MILKY WAY?
WOW! IT REALLY LOOKS LIKE SPILT MILK.
"CAMPANELLA, LET'S GO TOGETHER."
FROM THE BEAR'S BIBLE - KEN MIYAZAWA'S "TWIN STARS (FUTAGO NO HOSHI)"?
"THE GALAXY EXPRESS (GINGA TETSUDO)"
"THE WELL IN THE SKY, JUST PAST THE WEST BANK OF THE MILKY WAY."

I'M GOING TO KISS YOU.
I TOLD YOU NOT TO...
NO. BECAUSE YOU CAN'T CONTROL YOURSELF.

I HEARD YOU RESIGNED FROM TSUKISHIMA DOJO?

MASTER OHMORI TRIED TO STOP ME BUT I'VE GOT MY PRIORITIES.
I WON'T BE ABLE TO MAKE IT TO THE DOJO ANYMORE.

YOU WON'T EVER BE ABLE TO GIVE UP KENDO ALTOGETHER.

THAT'S DISAP-POINTING.

JUST COME ON BACK WHEN YOU'VE GOT THE TIME.
DON'T MAKE SUCH A SWEET FACE AT ME.
I SWEAR I'LL JUMP YOU!

WELL, I'LL HEAD BACK TO THE ROOM FIRST.
COME IN AFTER I'VE FALLEN ASLEEP, ALL RIGHT? AND MAKE SURE YOU WAKE UP BEFORE I DO TOMORROW MORNING.
I'M BEGGING YOU.
I FEEL LIKE I'M GOING TO FALL...
...INTO THE MILKY WAY...

"IT'S TOO LATE.
"IT'S ALREADY BEEN FORTY-FIVE MINUTES SINCE HE FELL IN."

I DON'T THINK I CAN DO IT.
THERE'RE A LOT OF REASONS BUT I JUST DON'T HAVE THE CONFI-DENCE.
THERE ARE HIGH SCHOOL STUDENTS OLDER THAN I AM, TOO...
BUT I THINK YOU'RE THE BEST MAN FOR THE JOB.
I CAN'T UNDERSTAND WHY YOU FEEL THAT WAY, MR. HANAMORI...
NO— GO...?
I THOUGHT HE'D BECOME MUCH MORE ASSERTIVE, BUT...
THAT'S THANKS TO MASAOMI.
THAT BAKA-OMI?
YEAH. MASAOMI ACTS AS A BRIDGE BETWEEN SAYA AND THE OTHER STUDENTS.

YESTERDAY, I WAS IN THE MOOD TO GIVE UP...
BUT RIGHT NOW, I COULD KILL YOU.
DON'T LOOK LIKE THAT. IT WAS A JOKE.
THE SUN'S COMING UP. LET'S HEAD BACK.
FOR THE NEXT-LEADER-IN-LINE AT OUR DOJO...
I WAS THINKING ABOUT PUSHING FOR YOUR KID BROTHER - WHAT DO YOU THINK?
I PUT HIM IN YOUR HANDS. TRAIN HIM WELL.
RING DING
GONG DONG
キーン コーン
カーン コーン
PRACTICE OVER!

...I'M STRUGGLING.
YOU KNOW SOMETHING, TSURUGI YAEGASHI?
EVER SINCE I MET YOU TWO YEARS AGO...
EVERY DAY, I'M CONSTANTLY ON THE VERGE OF BEING SWEPT AWAY BY SOME NEW EMOTION.
SOMETIMES IT'S HAPPINESS, SOMETIMES IT'S TRIUMPH...
OTHER TIMES IT'S THE COMPLETE OPPOSITE - ALL KINDS OF EMOTIONS.
MAYBE THERE'LL NEVER BE AN ANSWER.
AND WHAT ABOUT NOW...?

SHUFF
SHUFF
SHUFF
SHUFF
QUITE A VIEW...
I JOG UP HERE EVERY YEAR, JUST TO SEE THIS VIEW.
I WAS HESITANT ABOUT WHETHER OR NOT TO COME TO THIS TRAINING CAMP.
EVEN NOW...
BUT I WANTED TO KEEP STRUGGLING.
THE PHRASE "GRACEFUL DEFEAT" CAME IMMEDIATELY TO MIND.
WHEN YOU SHOWED ME THAT SWORD...

ぴちゃん
SPLOSH

君知るや

DOST THOU KNOW - PART 2

WHAAAT? YOU'RE AN IDIOT, OKINOSHIMA!
AND THAT'S WHAT HE SAID!
BUT HE CAN'T RELY ON MASAOMI FOREVER.
YOUR TOUGH-LOVE TACTICS... IT'S GOING TO BE A TRIAL FOR SAYA.
I'VE GOT TO...
... DECIDE FOR MYSELF ...
HEY, SAYA!
HUH?
HE WAS JUST THERE, WASN'T HE?
WHAAAT? MASAOMI, ARE YOU SEEING THINGS?
YOU'RE LOSING IT!
HA HA HA HA!

WHAP
CLATTER
HE DROPPED HIS SHINAI.
...
THAT'S THE THIRD TIME TODAY. WHAT'S WRONG WITH SAYA?
I'M SORRY...
IT'S BECAUSE YOU WEREN'T CONCEN-TRATING!
GO OUTSIDE AND GET SOME FRESH AIR!
HAA...

YOU'RE GOING TO TRAIN OVER HERE WITH ME.
AAAAAAAHHH
THAT'S NOT TRUE. THERE ARE A LOT OF THINGS I HAVEN'T FOUND THE ANSWER TO.
BUT I NEVER WANT TO HAVE ANY REGRETS.
THEN YOU DON'T REGRET HAVING TO QUIT KENDO, BIG BROTHER?
I BET YOU'D NEVER FALTER IN A SITUATION LIKE THIS...
I ENVY YOU.

I KNOW ABOUT IT... THAT NIGHT OF THE SUMMER FESTIVAL LAST YEAR.
YOU'VE BEEN RUNNING FROM MR. HANAMORI EVER SINCE.
AND THAT TIME WHEN YOU SLAMMED MR. HANAMORI OUT THROUGH THE DOORS OF THE DOJO...
THAT WAS BECAUSE YOU WERE AFRAID OF THINGS BEING SETTLED THEN AND THERE... WASN'T IT?
YOU WERE JUST PUTTING OFF REACHING A CONCLUSION...
AM I WRONG?
YOU COULD BE RIGHT...

SPLASH
SPLASH
ジャバシャ
HANA-MORI.
LET'S GO, SAYA.
LET'S GO REACH THE CON-CLUSION TOGETHER.
SORRY TO IMPOSE, BUT COULD YOU COME BACK TO THE GYM?
OH, MAN... OUR RIDE'S LATE.
I'M SUPER HUNGRY.
I WANNA GET BACK AND EAT THE LODGE LADY'S HOME-COOKED MEAL!

HEY, SOMETHING BIG'S GOING DOWN AT THE GYM!
WHOAA!
JEEZ!
HAD ENOUGH ?!
NOT YET!
LEAP

YOU STAMPEDING BOAR!
BAM
HEY... ISN'T THIS LIKE A DUEL?
SAYA...
THIS LOOKS BAD...
SOMEONE GO GET THE COACH.
WAIT!
R-RIGHT!
OKINOSHIMA, GO GET THE REFEREE'S FLAG!

YOU LOG-SPLITTER! YOUR SIDE IS WIDE OPEN!
....
WHAT?
QUIT FLITTING AROUND... STAND AND HOLD YOUR GROUND!
SOMEONE ACT AS THE SECOND REFEREE.
GOT IT!
KOJIMA, RECORD THE SCORE.
SLAM
OUT OF BOUNDS!
MASAOMI...

HAH HAH
HAH
YES!
WATER!
BEGIN!
HOW LONG ARE THEY GOING TO KEEP THIS UP...?
IT'S BEEN OVER AN HOUR ALREADY.
THOSE TWO ARE MONSTERS ...

ALL THE ILL FEELING...
...IS MELTING CLEAN AWAY.
ONE POINT!
HIS GRIP IS SLIPPING... I DON'T BELIEVE IT... THE SWEAT HAS SOAKED THROUGH TO THE OUTSIDE OF THE GAUNTLET!
SOME-ONE— GO GET A TOWEL!

I WISH I HAD DONE THIS...
...LONG BEFORE.
ZIPPO

剣
どたっ
THUD
I CAN'T- I CAN'T STAND UP ANYMORE...
ON YOUR FEET, HANAMORI!
HUFF
HUFF
HA HA HA...
YOU'RE ALL TALK...
SHUT UP! HUFF
WHEEZE HUFF
THANK YOU, BROTHER...

MR. HANAMORI, I LOVED YOU.
THANK YOU.
IN THE END, SAYA COMPLETED TRAINING CAMP AS THE NEXT APPOINTED LEADER...
AND HIS LAST MATCH, TSURUGI QUIETLY LAID HIS SHINAI TO REST.

WE'RE GOING OUT TO GET EVERYONE'S DINNER... WHAT WOULD YOU LIKE?
AN OPEN SANDWICH FROM JAKAMADO-YA.
OOOH, SIR SAYA HAS GROWN SO MATURE THIS SECOND SEMESTER.
I'M THINKING THERE'S SOME-THING BETWEEN HIM AND THE STUDENT COUNCIL VICE PRESIDENT, HANEGI.
SAYA...
2-2
IS THE SCHOOL FESTIVAL ACTIVITIES COUNCIL REPRESEN-TATIVE FOR THIS CLASS HERE?
IN ADDITION TO THE BUDGET WE REQUESTED, WE GOT THE SUPPORT OF THE TSUKISHIMA SHOPPING DISTRICT, SO...
WE'LL BE ALLOWING THE USE OF THESE COUPONS AT THE EVENT.
GOT IT. THAT'S SOME GOOD WORK, STUDENT COUNCIL PRESIDENT!
BE SURE EVERYONE LEAVES THE CAMPUS BY EIGHT-THIRTY AT THE LATEST.
WE'LL WRAP THINGS UP BY EIGHT.

WELL, I'VE BEEN PRETTY BUSY, WHAT WITH BEING LEADER AT THE DOJO AND STUDENT COUNCIL PRESIDENT...
WE REALLY HAVEN'T HAD A CHANCE TO TALK SINCE THE TRAINING CAMP.
I HEARD MR. HANAMORI WON IN THE INTER COLLEGE TEAM TOURNA-MENT?
LET'S WALK HOME TOGETHER, SAYA.
YEAH, CAN YOU BELIEVE IT? SOMEBODY STOP THAT RUNAWAY TRAIN!
HUH? DIDN'T YOU KNOW?
HOW'S MR. TSURUGI? IS HE WELL?
HE WAS OKAY THE LAST TIME I SAW HIM.
MY BROTHER MOVED OUT TO LIVE NEAR HIS COLLEGE.
WHAT?!
"THE LAST TIME"?
HUH?! MR. HANAMORI DOESN'T KNOW EITHER?!
OH, MAN... MY BRO'S GONNA BE DEPRESSED WHEN HE FINDS OUT...

YOU MUST BE LONELY, THEN. IF YOU NEED ANYTHING, LET ME KNOW.
DON'T SUFFER ALONE.
YOU CAN BE KIND ALL YOU WANT, BUT DON'T EXPECT ANYTHING IN RETURN.
WHA...! WHAT DO YOU MEAN, "IN RETURN"?!
SO, YOU'RE NOT EXPECTING ANYTHING, THEN?
WH- THAT'S- I'M...
YOU'RE SO GULLIBLE IT WAS JUST A JOKE.
WHY DON'T YOU GROW UP?
I'M PROBABLY GOING TO HAVE AN EVEN HARDER TIME THAN BRO DID...

*NOTE: PROTECTIVE TALISMANS

SUMMER IS ENDING...

SUCH A HOT SUMMER IT WAS...
SUMMER IS ENDING...
THE TROPIC LAND THAT DWELLS IN MY HEART.
I WONDER... WILL IT FADE AWAY AS WELL?

HANA-MORI...
WHY WON'T YOU CALL?
HUH?
YO.
I CAME TO GET OUR OMAMORI FOR TRAIN-ING CAMP.
I HAVEN'T SEEN YOU SINCE THE CAMP. IT'S BEEN TWO MONTHS...
YOU LOOK WELL.
... ...

WHAT?
DO I HAVE TO SPELL IT OUT FOR YOU?
DO I HAVE TO SAY IT? I SURRENDER.
THE CONCLUSION WAS REACHED LONG AGO.
ON THE NIGHT OF THE SUMMER FESTIVAL LAST YEAR...
...UNDER-NEATH THE FIRE-WORKS.

DOST THOU KNOW / END

HOW MANY YEARS HAS IT BEEEEEN??!!

I CAN ALMOST HEAR THESE WORDS BEING YELLED AT ME.

IT'S FINALLY OUT - "***DOST THOU KNOW***".

ABOUT THREE YEARS HAVE PASSED SINCE I WROTE THE FIRST CHAPTER. MANY THINGS HAVE HAPPENED SINCE THEN AND EVEN GRADUAL CHANGES TO MY ART STYLE CAN BE SEEN, BUT I AM HAPPY TO HAVE SUCCESSFULLY BROUGHT THE STORY TO ITS CONCLUSION. TO MY EDITOR "T", OTHERS, AND ALL YOU READERS WHO PATIENTLY STUCK WITH ME - THANK YOU ALL VERY MUCH.

MY ORIGINAL PLAN WAS TO SEPARATE THE STORY INTO SEASONS - SPRING, SUMMER, AUTUMN, AND WINTER - BUT FOR SOME REASON, THE LAST HALF TURNED OUT TO BE ALL SUMMER. AFTER ALL, THERE ARE SUMMER CAMPS, SUMMER FESTIVALS, THE BEACH, SUMMER VACATION - ALL PRIME EVENTS FOR PASSION TO ERUPT...BUT THE REAL REASON IS THAT IT WAS SUMMER WHEN I WAS WORKING ON THIS. IT WAS SO HOT...

SO - I DECLARE THAT, FROM NOW ON, I WILL PUT OUT GRAPHIC NOVELS AT A PACE OF ONE EVERY FOUR YEARS.

(KIDDING).

...OR AM I...?

DMP
Beyond My Touch
When a little thing like death gets in the way of love. A speacial ghost's affections, will come back from the beyond.
yaoi-manga.com
The girls only sanctuary
ISBN# 1-56970-928-9 $12.95
Beyond My Touch - Meniwa Sayakani Mienedomo © TOMO MAEDA 2003.
Originally published in Japan in 2003 by SHINSHOKAN Co., LTD

DMP
La Esperança
yaoi-manga.com
The girls only sanctuary
Despite young Georges popularity, he has never been able to truly forge a close bond with others. That is, of course, until he met Robert!
But after time, will Georges come to regret it?
Mystery surrounds him and only a tragic clue from the past may provide the answer.
La Esperança
Yaoi Manga
VOL. 1 ISBN# 1-56970-933-5 $12.95
VOL. 2 ISBN# 1-56970-932-7 $12.95
VOL. 3 ISBN# 1-56970-931-9 $12.95
VOL. 4 ISBN# 1-56970-930-0 $12.95
VOL. 5 ISBN# 1-56970-929-7 $12.95